The Pract
of Calvinism

A. N. MARTIN

Pastor of Trinity Baptist Church,
Essex Fells, New Jersey

THE BANNER OF TRUTH TRUST

THE BANNER OF TRUTH TRUST
3 Murrayfield Road, Edinburgh EH12 6EL
P.O. Box 621, Carlisle, Pennsylvania 17013, USA

*

© The Banner of Truth Trust 1979
First published 1979
Reprinted 1983
Reprinted 1988
Reprinted 1994

ISBN 0 85151 296 8

PRINTED BY BESHARA PRESS LTD., CHELTENHAM

The Experience of God

B. B. Warfield describes Calvinism as 'that sight of the majesty of God that pervades all of life and all of experience'. In particular as it relates to the doctrine of salvation its glad confession is summarized in those three pregnant words, *God saves sinners*. Now whenever we are confronted with great doctrinal statements in Holy Scripture, God does not leave us merely with the statement of doctrine. The end of God's truth set before the minds of God's people is that, understanding it, they might know its effect in their own personal experience. So the grand doctrinal themes of Ephesians, chapters 1, 2 and 3 are followed by the application of those doctrines to practical life and experience in Ephesians, chapters 4, 5 and 6. The end for which God gave his truth was not so much the instruction of our minds as the transformation of our lives. But a person cannot come directly to the life and experience, he must come mediately through the mind. And so God's truth is addressed to the understanding and the Spirit of God operates in the understanding as the Spirit of wisdom and knowledge. He does not illuminate the mind simply that the file drawers of the mental study may be crammed full of information. The end for which God instructs the mind is that he might transform the life.

What, then, are the personal implications of Calvinistic thought and truth both in the life of the individual and in the ministry exercised by the individual? By personal implications I mean the implications of your own relationship to God without any conscious reference to the ministry.

Now, these things cannot be separated in an absolute sense, for as has been well said, 'The life of a minister is the life of his ministry'. You cannot separate what you are from what you do; you cannot separate the effect of truth upon your own relationship to God personally from the effect of truth through you ministerially. For the sake of bringing the principles into sharp focus I am separating them, but in no way do I want to give the impression that these two are in rigid categories.

I ask then, What are the implications of Calvinistic thought, this vision of the majesty of God and of the saving truth of Scripture as it relates to us as individuals? In answer let us go back to that general principle which B. B. Warfield calls the 'formative principle of Calvinism'. I quote Warfield's words: 'It lies then, let me repeat, in a profound apprehension of God in His majesty, with the poignant realisation which inevitably accompanies this apprehension, of the relation sustained to God by the creature as such, and particularly by the sinful creature. The Calvinist is the man who has seen God, and who, having seen God in His glory, is filled on the one hand with a sense of his own unworthiness to stand in God's sight as a creature, and much more as a sinner, and on the other hand, with adoring wonder that nevertheless this God is a God who receives sinners. He who believes in God without reserve and is determined that God shall be God to him in all his thinking, feeling and willing – in the entire compass of his life activities, intellectual, moral and spiritual – throughout all his individual social and religious relations, is, by force of that strictest of all logic which presides over the outworking of principles into thought and life, by the very necessity of the case, a Calvinist.'[1]

Notice that when B. B. Warfield defines Calvinism and the Calvinist he used words of a strongly experimental nature.

[1]*Calvin as a Theologian and Calvinism Today.*

4

The words 'apprehension' and 'realisation' deal primarily with the understanding, though they go beyond that, but when we come to words such as 'seen God', 'filled on the one hand with a sense of his own unworthiness', 'adoring wonder', 'thinking, feeling and willing', these are words of experience. Warfield is really saying that no person is a Calvinist, no person is truly Biblical in his thinking of God, no man is truly religious, no man is truly evangelical until these concepts have been burned into the nerve fibres of his experience. In other words, Warfield would say that an academic Calvinist is a misnomer, as much as to speak of 'a living corpse' is a misnomer. When the soul and the body are separate death has taken place, and Warfield would teach us that when the soul of Calvinistic thought is dead or absent, all that remains is a carcase, a stench in the nostrils of God, and so often a stench in the church when found in a minister.

I

With this sort of background as to the personal implications, I want us next to consider a passage of Scripture, in which we have a historical account of how God makes a Calvinist. Turn to Isaiah, Chapter 6. 'In the year that king Uzziah died I saw also the Lord sitting upon a throne'. Isaiah, who knew king Uzziah well, and had seen him upon his throne, says that in the year that that king died he saw the true King. He mentions that again at the end of verse 5: 'for mine eyes have seen *the* King, the Lord of hosts'. And he saw him essentially as an *enthroned* king: 'I saw the Lord sitting upon a throne, high and lifted up, and his train filled the temple. Above it stood the seraphim: each one had six wings; with twain he covered his face, and with twain he covered his feet, and with twain he did fly. And one cried unto another, and said, Holy, holy, holy, is the Lord of hosts: the whole earth is full of his glory. And the posts of the door moved at the voice of him that cried, and the house was filled with smoke. Then said I, Woe is me! for I am undone; because I am a man of unclean lips, and I dwell in the midst of a people of unclean lips; for mine eyes have seen the King, the Lord of hosts. Then flew one of the seraphim unto me, having a live coal in his hand, which he had taken with the tongs from off the altar: And he laid it upon my mouth' – the sensitive tissues of the lips; a coal so hot that the seraph could not take it barehanded but had to take it with tongs. It sears the lips of the prophet. Then follow the words of comfort, 'Lo, this hath touched thy lips; and thine iniquity is taken away, and thy sin purged. Also I heard the voice of the Lord, saying, Whom shall I send, and who will go for us? Then said I, Here am I; send me. And he said, Go, and tell this people, Hear ye indeed, but understand not; and see ye indeed, but perceive not. Make the heart of this people fat, and make their ears heavy, and shut their eyes; lest they see with their eyes, and hear with their ears, and understand with their heart, and convert, and be healed. Then said I, Lord, how long? And he answered, Until the cities be wasted without inhabitant, and the houses without man, and the land be utterly desolate.'

Here is the record of how God makes a Calvinist, how God brought a man to a vision of the majesty of God that so affected him that his life was never the same again. The first thing that struck him in this vision was this sight of God as the high and the lofty One, seated upon a throne, so that whatever else is introduced into the vision – the holiness of God, the grace of God, the forgiveness of God – it is the shining forth of God from a position of enthrone-ment: 'I saw the Lord *sitting* upon a throne, high and lifted up'. So we may say rightly that it was sovereign holiness as well as a holy sovereignty that was exercised. It was sovereign grace as well as a gracious sovereignty. And this display of the Lord as the King brought with it several distinct results in the life of the prophet.

In the first place, *it brought a deep experimental acquaintance with his own sinfulness.* 'Woe is me! I am undone. I've been shocked. I've gone to pieces. I've fallen apart'. Now who was he? Was he some hippie yanked off the streets who had been holding up little four-lettered words to those who did not like his interests? Was he some kind of student who had been running around under the guise of the so-called insights of new morality giving bent to his animal passions? No, this was Isaiah, from all indication in the record of Scripture a holy man, a man of God, what would be termed a dedicated Christian. But he had yet to have a sight and vision of the Lord that shattered him and shook him and exposed the inherent corruption of his own heart and life. And I submit that God never makes Calvinists by displaying to them his glory and his majesty without bringing with it this commensurate exposure of sin in the light of his sovereignty and his holiness. It brought with it also a deep insight into the state of his own generation, for note that in his own confession he not only says, 'I am a man of unclean lips' but 'I dwell in the midst of a people of unclean lips'. In the record of the state of the people as found for example in Isaiah 58, we find that they were extremely religious; they came daily to the temple and offered sacrifices. Read Isaiah 1, and you will find the prophet's contemporaries bringing their sacrifices and keeping their feast days. Yet God said, 'I am sick and tired of the whole thing. Bring no more vain oblations . . . When you make many prayers I will not hear'. And if you and I had been standing there as onlookers we would have said that religion in Israel was in a pretty good state. But when this man had a sight and sense of the majesty of God, it brought with it not only an insight into his own sinfulness, but also into the state of his own generation.

Next *it brought an experimental acquaintance with grace and forgiveness*. As Isaiah feels his uncleanness, his undoneness in the presence of the Lord, the seraph takes a live coal from off the altar of sacrifice, a coal which becomes the symbol of the basis upon which God forgives sinners. It touches the lips of the prophet, and though there is inner pain, there is also that wonderful word of grace, 'Thine iniquity is taken away, and thy sin purged'. Here is a man who has been brought to the sight of his own sin in such a way that he wonders how it can be that such a person as he is can dwell in the presence of such a One as the Lord is. It is *that* person to whom the word of forgiveness is a humbling, overpowering, captivating word. The reason why grace is so little appreciated in our days is that the transcendent majesty and sovereignty and holiness of God are so little appreciated, and we do not see much more than a half step between God and our sinful selves. But Isaiah saw as it were an infinite chasm, and when the Lord sovereignly extended mercy across that chasm and touched him, he became a man who then evidenced the fruit of grace.

Thirdly, it tells us *of a man who was brought to utter resignation before God*. Having been purged, Isaiah next tells us, 'I heard the voice of the Lord saying, Whom shall I send, and who will go for us?' Note the prophet's reaction. Having seen the Lord in his sovereignty and holiness, and himself in his uncleanness, and having heard the word of grace and forgiveness, what can a man do when this Lord speaks and he hears His voice, but say, 'Here am I'. There is nothing here of the missionary telling tear-jerking stories about human sin and human need, in the attempt to wrench young people from their seat of complacency and rebellion to the revealed will of God and to get them to crank out an 'Here am I'. This was just the reflex action of a man who had seen the Lord and heard his voice, and he says,

'Here am I, Lord, send me'. And then, as it were, the Lord tests the depths of that confession and we find an utter resignation to the will and ways of the Lord, no matter how strange they seem, for it is immediately made clear to the prophet that he is to have a ministry primarily of judgment: 'Go, and tell this people, hear . . . and understand not; see . . . perceive not. Make the heart of this people fat'. 'Isaiah, I am commissioning you to a ministry of hardening and of judgment'. Now what does the prophet do? Does the prophet recoil and say, 'O Lord, that isn't fair. Do not call me to such a work as that'. No, no! He simply says, 'Lord, how long?' In other words, 'Lord, it is your perfect right to send me on a ministry which will be primarily a ministry of hardening and judgment. You are God. You are on the throne. I am the creature before the throne. You are holy. I am sinful. What can I do but be held captive by the expression of your will, no matter what the implications may be?'

This is how God makes a man a Calvinist. In one way or another he gives him such a sight of his own majesty and sovereignty and holiness as the high and the lofty One, that it brings with it a deep, experimental acquaintance with human sinfulness personally and in terms of our own generation. It brings experimental acquaintance with the grace of God, an intimate acquaintance with the voice of God, an utter resignation to the will and the ways of God.

II

I say by way of application, do not talk about being a Calvinist simply because your itch for logical consistency has been relieved by Calvinism's theological system. Have you seen God? Have you been brought near to Him? That is the issue. I remind you of the words of B. B. Warfield: 'A Calvinist is a man who has seen God'. The expression, a proud Calvinist, is a misnomer. If a Calvinist is a man who has seen God as He is high and lifted up, enthroned, then he is a man who has been brought to brokenness before that throne as was Isaiah. A carnal Calvinist? Another misnomer! The enthroned One is the holy One, and He dwells in conscious communion with those who are rightly related to Him as the enthroned One and as the holy One. These two things are brought together beautifully in Isaiah 57.15 where the prophet says: 'Thus saith the high and lofty One that inhabiteth eternity, whose name is Holy; I dwell in the high and holy place, with him also that is of a contrite and a humble spirit'. What is contrition? It is the reaction of a sinner in the presence of a holy God; and, what is humility? It is the reaction of a subject in the presence of a sovereign. Isaiah never forgot this vision, and he says, 'This great God dwells in that high and holy place, with him also that is of a humble and a contrite spirit, to revive the spirit of the humble, and to revive the heart of the contrite ones.'

If your understanding of Calvinistic thinking has led you to the place where you can, as it were, boast in your liberty and use it as an occasion for licence, then you have never become a biblical Calvinist. God makes Calvinists today the same way he made them in Isaiah's day.

I submit that a man has no right to speak of being a Calvinist because he can repeat like a parrot phrases brought to him in the great heritage of Reformed literature. He must ask himself, Has the Holy Spirit brought me to this profound sense of God that has worked in me at least in some measure the grace of humility. Has God endowed me with gifts and abilities? If so, what have I that I did not receive? Who makes me to differ? If God has endowed me with gifts and abilities whether intellectual or otherwise, I acknowledge that I have those because a Sovereign upon a throne was pleased to dispense them to me, and the only difference between me and that poor retarded child that moves the pity of my heart, is that He was pleased to make me different. 'Who maketh thee to differ?' The man who stands in the presence of a God upon the throne, and who has had this sight and sense of the majesty of God, recognizes that all that he has, has been given. Humility is not diffidence. Humility is that disposition of honest recognition: He is God, I am but a creature. All that I have comes from him and must be rendered to him in praise, and in honour. It will bring with it the submission that we see in Isaiah. He sits upon a throne; I have no rights to assert, but I have the unspeakable privilege of knowing and doing his will. Was not that the reflex action of Isaiah? The Lord is upon the throne; I am the creature. What else can I do but say, 'Here am I?'

Oh, the unspeakable delight of knowing and doing the will of God! It brings not only humility and submission, but true contrition, for I see then that all sin has been basically a violent anarchist spirit exerted against the throne-rights of God. Have I failed to love Him with the whole heart? Then this has been anarchy. He demands and is worthy of my undivided affection. Have I failed to love my neighbour as myself and given expression to this sin in a disrespect for parents, a disrespect for the rights and life of others, the purity and sanctity of others, the reputation of others? Go through the Ten Commandments, and learn that any breach of them is at its core violent anarchy against the throne-rights of God. All pride – what is it but an attempt to share the glory that belongs to the throne, and to the God upon that throne, and to say in reality, 'O God, please let me sneak into the picture and get glory too?' Is not that pride? – a wicked attempt to share the praise of the enthroned God!

And so this sight of God cannot help but produce humility, submission, contrition, and on the brighter side, it cannot help but produce gratitude, that in the exercise of His

11

sovereign rights I should be blessed of God with sanity, with soundness of body, clearness of mind, and, above all, that I should be blessed with grace, confidence that God is on His throne, that nothing past, present or future has ever made that throne twitter one-thousandth of an inch. Jehovah reigneth! let the earth tremble. Confidence, unshakable confidence, joy, regardless of what transpires in the sphere that I can see! All is well where He sits.

Has God made you a Calvinist? I am not asking whether you have read a book by Boettner, or Kuyper or Warfield and become a Calvinist. I am asking, Has God given you a vision of himself? Did He shatter you? and bring you to that place by his grace of humility, submission, contrition, gratitude, confidence and joy? That is what makes a Calvinist. If we know this we will want to say,

> My God, how wonderful Thou art,
>   Thy majesty how bright!
> How beautiful Thy mercy-seat,
>   In depths of burning light!
>
> O how I fear Thee, living God,
>   With deepest, tenderest fears,
> And worship Thee with trembling hope
>   And penitential tears!
>
> How beautiful, how beautiful
>   The sight of Thee must be,
> Thine endless wisdom, boundless power,
>   And awful purity!

The Power of Saving Religion

We now turn our attention to the specific soteriological aspects of Calvinism – the 'doctrines of grace'. I have already said that the *saving* aspects of biblical truth, commonly called Calvinism, would be the focus of our attention – the confession that *God saves sinners*. What effect should that have upon the life of an individual? Is Calvinism, essentially in the realm of soteriology, a declaration of the saving mercy of God exercised sovereignly and powerfully upon elect sinners? If so, then at the very core of Calvinistic, biblical thinking regarding salvation is this belief that God has taken the initiative, that God has done something, that God is [present tense] doing something. Warfield has this to say: 'There is nothing, therefore, against which Calvinism sets its face with more firmness than every form and degree of auto-soterism, every form of self-salvation. Above everything else it is determined to recognize God in his Son Jesus Christ acting through the Holy Spirit whom he has sent as our veritable Saviour.'

In the eyes of the Calvinist, sinful man stands in need, not of inducements or of assistance to save himself, but precisely of saving. He holds that Jesus Christ has come, not to advise, urge or woo, or to help a man to save himself, but to save him, to save him through the prevalent working in him of the Holy Spirit. This is the root of the Calvinistic soteriology.

Now if that is so, that at the root of Calvinistic soteriology is the confession that God saves sinners, accompanied as it is by a refusal to bleed any of the full meaning out of

13

any one of those words, it should lead in a very practical way to two things in the life of the individual.

I

First, it should lead to honest scriptural self-examination. I did not say unscriptural or neurotic introspection. And I believe that our fear of neurotic introspection has kept many of us in Reformed circles from honest, scriptural self-examination. By scriptural self-examination I mean a simple obedience to passages like 2 Corinthians 13.5, 'Examine yourselves, whether ye be in the faith; prove your own selves. Know ye not your own selves, how that Jesus Christ is in you, except ye be reprobates?' I mean obedience to the exhortation of 2 Peter 1.10, 'Give diligence to make your calling and election sure'. Similar words are found throughout the New Testament – 'Let no man deceive himself; let no man deceive you; be not deceived'. I am speaking of that scriptural duty.

It is obvious how this fits in as an implication of the Calvinistic concept of salvation. Since Scripture declares that all who are truly saved are the workmanship of God [*Eph* 2.10], then the question I must ask is, 'Have I been the subject of that workmanship?' The question is not the sincerity of my decision, or my resolve, or my whatever-I-want-to-call-it. The question is not, 'What have *I done* with reference to Christ and his salvation?' The essential question is this: 'Has God done something in me?' Not, 'Have I accepted Christ?' but, 'Has Christ accepted me?' The issue is not, 'Have I found the Lord?' but, 'Has he found me?'

One of the old masters in Israel used to ask those who aspired to be admitted to the table of the Lord, or to church membership, two questions. Firstly, 'What has Christ done *for* you?' He wanted to see if they understood the objective basis upon which God received sinners. He wanted to see

14

if they understood that men are accepted before God on the basis of the work of Jesus Christ plus nothing. And if it was clear to him that they did not think in any way that they were accepted by virtue of their repentance, their tears, their works, but solely upon the merits of Christ, then he would ask them the second question: 'What has Christ wrought *in* you?' You know what he has done *for* you, now my question is, What has he wrought *in* you? He asked that question because he understood the terrible possibility that a person might have an intellectual grasp of what Christ has done *for* sinners, and yet be an utter stranger to his mighty work *in* sinners.

And so I want to press some questions home to everyone's conscience. First: 'Have you been brought to see your own corruption in sin in such a measure that the first two beatitudes are true of you?' The only people in the world who are truly blessed are those who have been so wrought upon by the Spirit that they are not strangers to these two things: 'Blessed are the poor in spirit, for theirs is the kingdom of heaven. Blessed are they that mourn, for they shall be comforted'. How does God make men truly blessed, truly happy? First of all, he makes them sad at the sight and sense of their own impoverishment in a state of sin. What is poverty of spirit? Is it some kind of pseudo-pietistic attempt to convince myself that I am a miserable worm and a wretch? Not at all! Poverty of spirit results from just getting a sight of what you really are, and seeing that you *are* nothing and *have* nothing and *can do* nothing that can commend yourself to the grace and saving favour of God; it results from the conviction that he could make you an eternal monument of his righteous wrath, and let you perish in the eternal burning. Have you been brought to some experimental acquaintance with that? If not, I doubt whether you can claim that Christ is your Saviour, for he said that he came not to call the righteous but sinners to repentance. The poor in spirit have been made consciously aware of their depravity and sin.

It is possible to hold the doctrine of total depravity as a theological concept, and be as evil, proud and self-righteous as the devil. Have you known an inner stripping that has brought you to poverty of spirit? to holy mourning? to the recognition that your sin has been against the Sovereign God? Have you been brought to the place where you hate your sin enough to forsake it and cleave only to Christ? One old writer has beautifully said, 'When the Holy Ghost begins the chord of grace in the life of a man, he always orients that chord to the bass note'. He begins with the bass note of conviction, a revelation of our need of the Saviour. Have I been brought to see that unless He initiates the work it will never be done?

The next question I would ask is this: 'Do I evidence the fruit of his working?' And what is positive, undeniable evidence that God has been and is working in me? I would say without any fear of contradiction in the light of Holy Scripture that the evidence is biblical holiness. The so-called Five Points of Calvinism are cast in a negative form and can in some ways be misleading. Nonetheless we cannot change the course of history, and so the Five Points have come down to us and we must learn to live with them. Take the last four points – unconditional election, particular redemption [Christ died to save specific people], the efficacious call of God and the preserving work of God in all whom he has called and joined to his Son: What is the focal point in all of these? The ultimate focal point, of course, is the display of the glory of God's grace, as we read in Ephesians 1; but as the immediate focal point, how is that glory displayed? by what means? By the taking of totally depraved creatures and making them wholly men and women in whom the very likeness of God's Son can be seen. What is the goal of election? Ephesians 1.4 tells us: 'According as he hath chosen us in him before the foundation of the world, that' . . . we should glory in our election? No! But 'that we should be holy and without blemish before him'. Election *unto* holiness! What is the goal of the atoning work of Christ? Listen to the testimony of Titus 2.14: 'Who gave himself for us, that he might redeem us from all iniquity, and purify unto himself a people as his distinct possession, zealous of good works'. He died to have a holy people 'zealous of good works'.

Then there is the efficacious call of God, 'God is faithful, by whom ye were called unto the fellowship of his Son Jesus Christ our Lord' [1 *Cor* 1.9]. 'Called into a life of sharing vital realized communion with Christ!' 'For God hath not called us unto uncleanness, but unto holiness' [1 *Thess* 4.7].

Again, there is the preservation and perseverance of the saints. It is a perseverance in the ways of holiness and obedience, for Scripture says, 'Follow after holiness without which no man shall see the Lord' [*Heb* 12.14]. 'If ye continue in my word, then are ye my disciples indeed, and ye shall know the truth and the truth shall make you free' [*John* 8.31, 32]. And so wherever we touch any part of the structure of Calvinistic soteriology we touch a living fibre of God's purpose to have a holy people.

Predestinated to what end? 'Whom he foreknew he did predestinate to be conformed to the image of his Son' [*Rom* 8.29]. If so, then I must ask a question of myself: Is God's electing purpose being realized in me? He chose me in Christ that, being purchased in time and called in time, I might begin to be holy in time, and have that work perfected in eternity. The only assurance I have that I was purchased to be holy, and will be perfected in holiness, is that I am pursuing holiness here and now. Essentially holiness is conformity to the revealed will of God in thought, word and deed, through the power of the Holy Spirit and through union with Jesus Christ. Holiness, godliness, this is the evidence that his electing purpose has come to life and fruition and it finds its expression in obedience. That is why John can say in 1 John 2.5, 'Whoso keepeth his word, in him verily is the love of God perfected'. It finds its designed end in the one who keeps the Word of God. Is there clear evidence that I am experiencing communion with Jesus Christ through his Word? For he has called me into fellowship with himself, and if I have been effectually called then I am no stranger to experimental acquaintance with the Lord.

Do I confess that I am being preserved by God's keeping power? Then his preserving must be coming to light in my persevering. The only proof I have that he preserves me is that by his grace, I am enabled to persevere.

This is the practical implication of Calvinistic soteriology. It makes me ask questions like these which bring me into the whole context of honest scriptural self-examination. John Bunyan was right on target when he wrote that section in his immortal *Pilgrim's Progress* which describes how Christian and Faithful come into contact with a man named Talkative.[2] I urge you to read it carefully. It shows that Bunyan recognized that there is such a thing as having an intellectual conviction that only God can save sinners, and that salvation is a work in which God *saves* sinners, but the real issue is this, Has there been an experimental application of that truth with power to my own heart and to my own life?

About a year ago, a young man, a Seminary graduate, came to me, to talk about some matters that were disturbing him about my own ministry. He asked me this question, 'Mr Martin, I want to ask you a simple question. Do you believe that you have a calling to go round the country getting people upset?' I answered: 'My calling is not to

[2] *Pilgrim's Progress*, pp 81-95, Banner of Truth Trust.

go round the country getting people upset, but I am called to declare the whole counsel of God, one aspect of which focusses upon this principle, that it is possible to hold the form of sound words and yet to be lost and undone and a stranger to grace; for the Scripture says, "The kingdom of God is not in word but in power". Paul said, "Our gospel came not in word only but in power and in the Holy Ghost and in much assurance". As long as Matthew 7.21-23 stands in Holy Scripture, and as long as I have a voice, I shall cry out to ministers and potential ministers and professing Christians that many will say in that day, "Lord, Lord", to whom Christ will say, "Depart from me. I never knew you".'

I would never want to be an unwitting instrument of the devil to unsettle the faith of a true child of God who may be like Bunyan's Mr Ready-to-halt or Mr Fearing, or Mr Feeble-Mind, men who are on their way to the Celestial City but who have problems about assurance and who are doubting and failing. I would never be an accuser of the brethren to destroy or hurt the faith of a true Christian. But neither would I be a dumb dog, silent on the issue, that it is not enough to have inherited a form of doctrine, whether it be Calvinistic or Arminian. The issue is this: If salvation is of the Lord, has he begun a work in me? So I submit that these doctrines applied to the heart will lead to honest scriptural self-examination.

II

In the second place, these doctrines will lead to the sane biblical pursuit of practical godliness. What is involved in such a pursuit? To be brief, three things:

1. *A holy watchfulness and distrust of oneself.* Do I really believe that by nature I am so undone that God must initiate the work, and that the remains of corruption

in me, even after I have been regenerated and joined to Jesus Christ, are such that if God took his hand off me for a moment, they would lead me back into every form of wickedness possible to a human being? Such a belief will produce a holy watchfulness and a wholesome distrust of myself. If I recognize that the corruption that remains within me is like a dry tinderbox and that every temptation is like a live coal, I shall not dare to flirt with sin. If I have come out of perhaps a narrow fundamentalistic background with its checklist morality, and I discover the glorious truth of liberty in Christ, I shall not use my liberty as an opportunity for licence. I will recognize that I am free in Jesus Christ, and yet that I am one who has this terrible potential to wickedness within me, and I shall watch as well as pray.

2. *A consistent prayerfulness.* Is salvation the Lord's work from beginning to end? Then he must help, and his help is given to those who cry out to him. He must work in me to will and to do of his good pleasure, and I must *ask* him to do it. The Word shows the beautiful fusion of those two things: God's covenant promise to do something sovereignly and powerfully, joined with his command to his people to ask him for the very thing he has pledged to do. In Ezekiel 36, that expanded statement of the blessings of the new covenant, God makes great assertions [see verses 25 to 36] and yet in verse 37 we read: 'Thus saith the Lord God; I will yet for this be inquired of by the house of Israel, to do it for them'; '*I* will do it'; 'I will be inquired of'. In the economy of grace God awakens in the heart of those to whom he would dispense them the desire for the blessings which sovereignly and powerfully he engages to dispense. Matthew Henry, in his simple, homely, quaint way, says, 'When God deigns to bless his people he sets them a-praying for the blessing which he desires to give them'. And so, if I believe the confession that *God saves*

20

sinners, that he not only regenerates them, bringing them to repentance and faith, but that he keeps them and ultimately brings them into his presence – if that is *his* work then it will produce a consistent prayerfulness, not only a holy watchfulness and distrust of myself, but a constant application to him that he would perform in me that which he has promised. For what is prayer in the last analysis? It is a conscious spreading out of my helplessness before God. The true Calvinist is the man who confesses with his lips that grace must not only awaken him, regenerate him, but that grace must preserve him, and he Amens his confession by his prayer when on his knees he cries out, 'Lead me *not* into temptation but deliver me from evil. I cannot even get my bread for today, Lord, unless you sustain my life and bless the labours of my hands: Give me this day my daily bread'. The doctrine of confession, God saves sinners, will produce in the heart of a true Christian the sane biblical pursuit of godliness, holy watchfulness, a consistent prayerfulness, and in the third place:

3. *A trustful dependence on God to fulfil all that he has purposed.* When I sin, am I cast away? No! The word of God is, 'A just man falleth seven times and riseth up again' [*Prov* 24.16]. And so I come acknowledging that my obedience is neither the basis for my justification nor the ground of my approach to God as a sinner who has been besmeared by sin, and I flee afresh to the Mediator of the New Covenant. Peter puts the matter of recourse to the Lord in the present tense, 'To whom coming . . .' not 'to whom ye came'. So often in our day we hear it said that 'somebody *came* to Christ'. A Christian is a man who is *ever* coming. We read in Hebrews 12, 'Ye are not come . . .' and then he describes some of the physical surroundings that we get in the Old Covenant, but he says, 'Ye are come to . . .' and he mentions all the blessings of the New Covenant, and one of them is this: 'Ye are come . . . to Jesus the mediator

21

of the new covenant'. 'If any man sin we have [present tense] an advocate with the Father, Jesus Christ the righteous.'

Is not this why a true Christian does not cringe at the exposure of his sin? Every exposure of sin in the life of a true believer drives him afresh to his Saviour, and anything that drives him afresh to his Saviour makes his Saviour more precious. When is your life more fragrant than when the kiss of forgiveness is most fresh upon your cheek? Sin felt and mourned over drives a Christian afresh to the Mediator of the New Covenant who knew all about his failures when he called him, and in his grace and mercy as a suffering High Priest ever pleads the merits of his blood before the Father. And so there is a trusting dependence upon God to fulfil all his purposes. When I am weak I need to remember that he prays for me. He said to Peter, 'Satan hath desired to have thee to sift thee as wheat. But I have prayed for thee that thy faith fail not. I did not pray that your courage fail not. Your courage will fail, Peter, but I have prayed that your faith fail not'. And even in Peter's denial there was not a casting-off of his faith. For the work which God's goodness began, the arm of his strength will complete. He will carry it on until the day of Jesus Christ.

For a person to claim to be a Calvinist, confessing the soteriological creed that God saves sinners, without this holy watchfulness, some measure of consistent prayerfulness, and a trusting dependence upon God in Christ to fulfil all that he, in grace, has promised, is a contradiction of terms. One of the great cries that is raised today, and some of it has justification, is that people, especially young men, who get hold of Calvinism, and seem to view it as an unanswerable, unassailable philosophical system, become proud, go back now to their secular schools and in ten minutes shoot holes in the views of their Professor of

Philosophy. They become proud, cocky. That is a caricature, that is not real Calvinism.

What is the personal practical effect of the confession of Calvinism in the life of a man? If he sees God, it will break him, and if he understands that God saves sinners, it will make him a trustful, prayerful, watchful person pursuing practical godliness. Is that what these doctrines are doing for you right where you sit this morning? Some, perhaps, to whom these things are new have feared them and said, 'Oh, that stuff will just lead to spiritual barrenness and dryness'. It is not so! For these are the truths of God's Word; I am convinced they are. In their totality they are the truth which is according to godliness, the truth that sanctifies us in answer to the prayer of our great High Priest. May God grant that the truth will do that in you and in me!

A LIFE OF PRINCIPLED OBEDIENCE

Albert N. Martin

Based on the words of Psalm 119: 57-60, *A Life of Principled Obedience* expounds the essential elements of faithful Christian living. Bringing a life-time of pastoral experience to bear on this important subject, Albert N. Martin explains the foundation on which an obedient Christian life is built, the context in which it develops and the blessing to which it leads. Profoundly challenging, this biblical teaching also points to the true freedom and joy of authentic Christian living.

ISBN 0 85151 643 3
32pp. Booklet

FIVE POINTS OF CALVINISM

W. J. Seaton

By an accident of history in the 17th Century five great Christian truths, formulated by successors of the Reformers at the Synod of Dort to counter a drift from the gospel, became linked with the name of the Genevan Reformer who had died half a century earlier. The label 'Calvinism' was at first a propaganda tactic on the part of the opponents, but while defenders of the Reformation Faith recognised that it could well be called by another name they came to accept the term as denoting those doctrines which place man in entire dependence upon the free grace of God in salvation.

Since the Reformation there have been eras when Calvinism, apparently discredited and forgotten, has risen again with vital force and evangelical power. If that is happening, as it appears today, then it means that biblical teaching is once more coming to the fore. This present booklet is written to explain that teaching, and the author's standpoint is the same as that of C.H. Spurgeon who once wrote:

'We believe in the five great points commonly known as Calvinistic; but we do not regard these five points as being barbed shafts which we are to thrust between the ribs of our fellow-Christians. We look upon them as being five great lamps which help to irradiate the cross; or, rather, five bright emanations springing from the glorious covenant of our Triune God, and illustrating the great doctrine of Jesus crucified.'

ISBN 0 85151 264 X
20pp. Booklet

THE SOVEREIGNTY OF GOD

A. W. Pink

Present day conditions, writes the author, 'call loudly for a new examination and new presentation of God's omnipotence, God's sufficiency, God's sovereignty. From every pulpit in the land it needs to be thundered forth that God still lives, that God still observes, that God still reigns. Faith is now in the crucible, it is being tested by fire, and there is no fixed and sufficient resting place for the heart and mind but in *the Throne of God*. What is needed now, as never before, is a full, positive, constructive setting forth of the Godhood of God.'

ISBN 0 85151 133 3
160pp. Paperback

LIVING THE CHRISTIAN LIFE

Albert N. Martin

Have you ever asked, perhaps in a sense of near-despair, 'How can I live the Christian life fruitfully and victoriously?

Since you often seem to fail so miserably, shouldn't you listen more carefully to teaching which promises you 'Life with a capital L'?

Shouldn't you follow the 'secrets' of spiritual living which promise to change you from being a 'struggler' to becoming an 'over-comer'?

Albert N. Martin faces these questions and answers them squarely from Scripture. He lays down six major principles of genuine spiritual experience, exposes unbalanced and counterfeit teaching, and builds a secure foundation for Christ-centred living.

Written in the vivid, direct and popular style which has made his preaching so widely appreciated and respected, Dr. Martin's *Living the Christian Life* contains a vital message for every Christian today.

ISBN 0 85151 493 X
32pp. Booklet

WHAT'S WRONG WITH PREACHING TODAY

Albert N. Martin

The Christian church today stands in need of a recovery of good preaching. But how is that to take place? Part of the remedy lies in seeking to answer the question, What has gone wrong with preaching? The ability to analyse the weaknesses of contemporary preaching (and preachers) is essential to developing healthy and fruitful preaching.

In answering this vital question, Dr. A.N. Martin draws on his own experience as a pastor and preacher and on the widespread opportunities he has had to teach and counsel other preachers. Fundamentally, however, his response is rooted in the biblical teaching on the character of those who preach and the message they are to proclaim. *What's Wrong with Preaching Today?* contains a searching message which will disturb complacency; but rather than create despair, it challenges all who preach (as well as those who hear) to rise to new levels of faithfulness and usefulness in the service of Christ.

ISBN 0 85151 632 7
32pp. Booklet

THE THOUGHT OF GOD

Maurice Roberts

This is a collection of articles which have already been widely read and appreciated as editorials in *The Banner of Truth* magazine, of which Maurice Roberts is the editor. Pointedly biblical, they are thoughtful and searching, humbling and exalting, challenging and encouraging.

Like editorials in other journals, Maurice Roberts' articles have spoken to the needs of the times. But while many editorials appear to have only historical or sociological interest at a later date, in contrast these are of lasting value. They have God and his Word as their starting place; and their horizon stretches beyond time to eternity. Those who have already read them will rejoice to have these pieces conveniently and permanently in book form, while those who come to them for the first time will appreciate their freshness, relevance and power, and will find in them a seriousness which has a sanctifying effect on the heart and a clarifying influence on the spiritual vision.

ISBN 0 85151 658 0
256pp. Paperback

For further details and a free illustrated catalogue please write to:
THE BANNER OF TRUTH TRUST
3 Murrayfield Road, Edinburgh EH12 6EL
P.O. Box 621, Carlisle, Pennsylvania, 17013, U.S.A.